About the Author

Elected to the Major League Baseball Hall of Fame in 1994, PHIL RIZZUTO is one of the most beloved players in the history of the New York Yankees. Known as "the Scooter," Rizzuto's fielding and bunting abilities, along with his personality, played critical roles in the great Yankee teams of the 1940s and early 1950s. In 1950, he won the Most Valuable Player Award. After retirement in 1956, Rizzuto moved into the broadcast booth and called Yankee games for forty years, becoming known for his colorful shout, "Holy cow!" Fans across the nation mourned his death on August 13, 2007, at age eighty-nine.

About the Editors

TOM PEYER has written many comic books, including Stephen Colbert's *Tek Jansen* and *Bart Simpson*. He has contributed short humor pieces to Slate and cartoons to the *Syracuse New Times*. He lives in Seattle.

HART SEELY is a reporter for the *Syracuse Post-Standard*. His humor pieces have appeared in *The New Yorker*, Slate, the *New York Times*, and on National ʳ ᵘᵇⁱᶜ ᴿᵃᵈⁱᵒ. He has edited and authored sever~~l books~~ ~~~~, New York.

O Holy Cow!

O Holy Cow!

The Selected Verse of Phil Rizzuto

Edited by Tom Peyer and Hart Seely

With a Foreword by Bobby Murcer

and an Introduction by Roy Blount, Jr.

AN **ecco** BOOK

HARPER

NEW YORK • LONDON • TORONTO • SYDNEY

*To my brother Pete and his son Bob, two of
baseball's mightiest. —T.P.*

To Hart, Kyle, and Madeline. —H.S.

HARPER

O HOLY COW! Copyright © 2008 by The Phil Rizzuto Estate. Foreword © 2008 by
Bobby Murcer. Introduction to the 1993 edition © 1993 by Roy Blount, Jr. Origi-
nal Editors' Note, "Scooter at the Bat," and Afterword © 2008 by Tom Peyer and
Hart Seely. All rights reserved. Printed in the United States of America. No part of
this book may be used or reproduced in any manner whatsoever without written
permission except in the case of brief quotations embodied in critical articles and
reviews. For information address HarperCollins Publishers, 10 East 53rd Street, New
York, NY 10022.

HarperCollins books may be purchased for educational, business, or sales promo-
tional use. For information please write: Special Markets Department, HarperCollins
Publishers, 10 East 53rd Street, New York, NY 10022.

FIRST EDITION

Designed by Justin Dodd

Library of Congress Cataloging-in-Publication Data

Rizzuto, Phil, 1917–2007.
  O holy cow! : the selected verse of Phil Rizzuto / edited by Tom Peyer and Hart
Seely; forword by Bobby Murcer; introduction by Roy Blount, Jr.—1st Ecco/Harper
expanded paperback.
     p. cm.
  This new and expanded edition includes sixty-six new, previously unpublished
poems.
ISBN 978-0-06-156713-1
1. New York Yankees (Baseball team)—Poetry. 2. Baseball—Poetry. I. Seely, Hart. II.
Peyer, Tom. III. Title.
  PS3568.I86O15 2008
  811'.54—dc22
  2007044899

08 09 10 11 12 ID/RRD 10 9 8 7 6 5 4 3 2 1

Contents

Contents

Contents

Contents

Foreword

My Friend, the Poet

Funny thing, I sat next to Phil Rizzuto in the broadcast booth for six years, and he and I played a ton of golf at charity events over the years, and yet I have to admit that I never, ever suspected Scooter of being a poet, at least not until after his first book of verse—*this* book—came out in 1993.

This little volume, now being reissued in a commemorative edition, demonstrates how much I *didn't* know about my dear friend and colleague. Can't help but think of that old kids' refrain when somebody accidentally made a rhyme:

> He's a poet
> And don't know it.
> But his feet show it—
> They're Longfellows.

(By the way, that's pretty much where my exposure to poetry ended until I took a seat next to Scooter up in the booth at Yankee Stadium.)

So all those times that Phil would come out with something out of left field and then turn to me and say, "So what do you think, Murcer?" That was just Phil road-testing a new sonnet. And those many occasions when he'd leave the booth after the seventh inning to "grab a cup of coffee" or "stretch his legs"? I now figure it was because he felt he did some of his best poetizing on the George Washington Bridge heading back to his New Jersey home and his beloved Cora.

A lot of the poems that follow will make you laugh out loud. Many will make you scratch your head, as for instance "Colorado," presented here in its entirety:

They're having more snow
Out in Colorado.
Which is not in Montana.
But it is not far from Montana.

But there's one—my favorite—that I guarantee will make you cry. Scooter "wrote" it on August 6, 1979. That was the terrible day the Yankees flew out to Canton, Ohio, in the morning to bury our Captain and my best friend, Thurman Munson, and then flew back to play the Orioles in Yankee Stadium. (The Captain wouldn't have had it any other way.) Scooter's poem that night is called "The Man in the Moon." Here are the last two stanzas:

You know, it might,
It might sound a little corny,
But we have the most beautiful full moon tonight.
And the crowd,
Enjoying whatever is going on right now.
They say it might sound corny,

But to me it's some kind of a,
  Like an omen.

Both the moon and Thurman Munson,
Both ascending up into heaven.
I just can't get it out of my mind.
I just saw that full moon,
And it just reminded me of Thurman.
  And that's it.

I didn't hear Scooter deliver this poem, of course, because I was down on the field. And while I heard about what he'd said later, I never saw his words turned into a poem until I picked up this book, *O Holy Cow!*

You'll find the whole poem on page 16, and you'll also find it in my own book, *Yankee for Life*, which comes out on my birthday (May 20) in 2008. It means that much to me, especially now that Phil is gone.

"Holy Cow! A guy who writes poetry without even knowing it? Hey, White, is there a Hall of Fame for poets?"

Scooter, we all miss you.

—BOBBY MURCER
2008

Introduction to the **1993** *Edition*

If the Scooter ever makes it
To the Baseball Hall of Fame,
As I believe he should,
My own closest brush with diamond
Immortality will be
The flu he had once
When I interviewed him.
He got it "from that Coleman,"
He said, meaning the old Yankee
Second-sacker Gerry.
And then
I came down with it.
Score that 4 to 6 to me—
One of my greatest sports thrills.

As to whether my verse is catching
Any quality of his,

note that I am throwing up my hands now and sliding into prose. Certainly my lines on how he gave me the flu are not in the same league as his on how he gave Yogi Berra squirrels

("Squirrels").[1] Mine on getting a bug, to put it another way, lack both the quickness and the range of the Scooter's on getting butterflies, ("Field of Butterflies").

How does he do it? You can't steal first base, baseball people say, but Rizzuto obviates the intentional fallacy. Less self-consciously even than a Homer,[2] he broadcasts his poetry orally and leaves the writing-down to less immanent[3] sensibilities. The Scooter's lyricism springs not from any imperative to advance literary tradition but from a half century of familiarity with baseball's various means of transmission: for instance, wood. In "DiMaggio's Bat,"[4] Rizzuto conveys DiMaggio's understanding of wood:

Being an old fisherman
He knew about the trees.

What I just did there was hop and scramble into position to quote one of my favorite Rizzuto passages, and did I ever do it awkwardly. Whereas Rizzuto can go from Dickie Thon to

---

1. When Berra and he were roommates, the Scooter told me in another interview, he would get Yogi to sleep by reading him bedtime stories.

2. One definition of a homer is a sports commentator who shamelessly favors the home team.

3. Is that not exactly the word I have in mind? To quote Scooter himself: *No? / No kiddin'? / Great.*

4. No homer jokes here.

Puerto Rico to World War II to Velarde to Stankiewicz ("Dickie Poem Number One"), with an easy rhythm. Well, not *easy*. Let me try to put it this way:

> They called him Scooter
> For his movement on the field,
> Picking up grounders
> And laying down bunts
> And running them out.
> And so does his mind scoot,
> As did that of
> William Carlos Williams,
> Who wrote:

> > *. . . you have it over a troop*
> > *of artists—*
> > *unless one should scour the world—*
> > *you have the ground sense necessary.*

> Scooter had the ground sense,
> All right,
> And it transferred to the booth,
> And it took to the air,
> And it fascinates millions;
> And now here it is
> Looking good on paper.
> What boots it that we scour the world
> Or at least the left side
> Of the infield

For artistry any further?

Great poet.

(As the Scooter himself says
Of Walden.)

Great great poet.

—Roy Blount, Jr.

Original Editors' Note

I have nothing to say, and I am saying it, and that is poetry.
                                                    —JOHN CAGE

Strange as these words may sound, I often play with the idea that when all the social theories collapse, and wars and revolution leave humanity in utter gloom, the poet—whom Plato banned from his Republic—may rise up to save us all.
                                          —ISAAC BASHEVIS SINGER

The golden years have slipped by me, but you gotta hang in there. A little low. Two balls and a strike.
                                                —P. F. RIZZUTO

For nearly four decades, P. F. Rizzuto has called play-by-play for a fictional baseball organization called the New York Yankees.

During this epoch of imagination, the self-described "Scooter" has enchanted students of life with poetic tales of dazzling no-hitters and dramatic home runs, detailing first-hand the psychoactive stream of feasts, birthday greetings, and celebrities that continually flashes through his mind, or as Mr. Rizzuto calls it, "the broadcast booth."

Here is the first collection of verses from the Bard of Baseball. Each selection appears exactly as it was conceived and spoken by Mr. Rizzuto during the metamorphic heat of a Yankee game. These masterpieces range from primal wail celebrations for home runs to gut-wrenching indictments of the cruel passage of time; from a richly endowed compliment to the cut of Willie Randolph's jib to a tinderbox condemnation of the cut of Luis Polonia's hair. In this magical otherworld, all Yankees are heroes, and all heroes live forever. Yea, it may be Kevin Maas striding to the plate, but be assured that it shall be Joe DiMaggio's bat under discussion in the booth.

Baseball historians recall Mr. Rizzuto's thirteen-year playing career for a dogged pursuit of perfection in the arts of fielding, running, and bunting. In 1950 he was honored as the Most Valuable Player in the American League. Six years later, after his aging frame could no longer function with gyroscopic precision, Mr. Rizzuto retired from athletic competition. From then on, he channeled his legendary physical discipline into an exploration of mind and mouth. Soon, he had perfected a unique ability to snatch the bad hops of reality in the webbing of his psyche, then fire them home, just in time to cut down the demons that sought to circle our baseless lives. They were out. We were safe.

Today, just as he once relayed the ball, P. F. Rizzuto now relays the Truth.

In this modern world, where leaders peddle false trust, where video masquerades as literacy, and where the dreams of common man are framed in thirty-second beer commercials, truth is hard to know.

But you can hear it coming from one man's broadcast booth.

He is shouting, "Holy Cow!"

We better listen.

—April 1993

Acknowledgments

We tell ya . . .
We'd like to thank the following folks
For wisdom and guidance:
There's Jeff Z. Klein, the planner,
And Chris Kingsley, the editor,
And WPIX, and the *Village Voice*,
The Miley Collection, Danrick Enterprises,
And Seaver, and White, and Murcer,
And all the New York Yankees,
And Cora, and certainly, most of all . . .
The greatest Yankee shortstop to ever do poetry.
(Assuming Jeter doesn't take up the pen.)
Forever in our hearts.
Number 10, the one and only.
Unbelievable.

—HART SEELY AND TOM PEYER

O Holy Cow!

Field of Butterflies

Absolutely!
If you don't get a little,
A few butterflies,
No matter what you do,
On the first day of anything,
You're not human.

> April 12, 1991
> New York at Kansas City
> Storm Davis pitching to Steve Sax
> First inning, no outs, bases empty
> (First batter, opening day)
> No score

Alienation

I think my head shrinks a little
In this indoor stadium.

I am ...

The mike is getting bigger.
And I have to tighten it.

> May 2, 1987
> New York at Minnesota
> Tommy John pitching to Al Newman
> Third inning, two outs, two base runners
> Yankees lead 3—2

Phil Rizzuto

To Be Alone

Hey White
You know where your loyalties are?

Right here.
The old pinstripes.

No.

You never wore them.
So you have a right to sing the blues.

> May 12, 1987
> Chicago at New York
> Bill Long pitching to Dan Pasqua
> Second inning, no outs, bases empty
> White Sox lead 1—0

On the Couch with Myself

I wonder if they work
Like the regular psychologists
And psychiatrists
Where you do all the talking
And they just listen
And nod.

> April 12, 1991
> New York at Kansas City
> Mark Davis pitching to Steve Sax
> Ninth inning, two outs, bases empty
> Royals lead 9–5

Phil Rizzuto

Chaos

This is very interesting.
Forget the game.
Right here.
Here's a guy can't see.
All right,
Gene Larkin is the NO!
Gene Larkin?
What did he do?
Base on balls.

> June 22, 1991
> Minnesota at New York
> Wade Taylor pitching to Shane Mack
> Sixth inning, two outs, one base runner
> Twins lead 2–0

Time and Money

Oh! TIME! No! TIME!
Puckett had asked for time!
Puckett had asked for time!
And the plate umpire was on the ball.

Remember the time that cost Don Money
A grand slam home run in Milwaukee?

See him there.
He's holding the hand.
That's when he asked for it.
And everybody's watching,
The pitcher and the runner,
Didn't see him call . . .
Time!

> May 8, 1987, WPIX–TV
> New York at Minnesota
> Dennis Rasmussen pitching to Kirby Puckett
> A pickoff attempt at second base
> Top of the first, one out, no count, no score
> Final: Twins 2, Yankees 0

Phil Rizzuto

My Secret

When I'm driving
To Yankee Stadium and back,
I do it so often.

I don't remember passing lights.
I don't remember paying tolls
Coming over the bridge.

Going back over the bridge,
I remember . . .

> August 19, 1992
> Oakland at New York
> Mike Moore pitching to Mel Hall
> Fifth inning, one out, bases empty
> Yankees lead 4–1

And On It Goes

To me,
Days are . . .
One is just like

Another.

I can't figure
What day it is.
What month.

>August 9, 1992
>Boston at New York
>Joe Hesketh pitching to Charlie Hayes
>First inning, two outs, bases empty
>Yankees lead 3—0

Phil Rizzuto

From Slumber I Heard the Men at Work

I.
Friday,
When I was forced
To leave the game after six innings,
You know,
I almost came back in the 13th inning,
Moore.
I want you to know I was thinking
Of Murcer and Seaver there.

II.
I woke up,
And it was like,
Like a nightmare.
I said,
"Could the game still be going on?"
And sure enough.
I started to get dressed.
And then the 14th inning came.
If it had gone another inning,
I'd have been there.

> August 30, 1992
> New York at Minnesota
> Russ Springer pitching to Chili Davis
> Sixth inning, two outs, bases empty
> Twins lead 5–1

Hero or the Goat

All right this is it,
The whole season coming down
To just one ball game,
And every mistake will be magnified,
And every great play will be magnified,
And it's a tough night for the players,
I'll tell ya.
I know last night,
Being in the same situation many times
With the great Yankee teams of the past,
You stay awake,
And you dream,
And you think of what might be,
If you are the hero or the goat.

October 14, 1976
AMERICAN LEAGUE EAST PLAYOFF
Final game
Kansas City at New York
Pre-game show

Phil Rizzuto

Imagine

One ball two strikes on Nettles,
Every pitch and every play
So important in this ball game.
Imagine two teams
Coming down to the end of the season,
Both winning 99 games,
Everybody thought 95 would win the pennant.
And it all boils down
To this one playoff game.
All right, Torrez ready.
The one-two pitch . . .

October 2, 1978
American League East Playoff
New York at Boston
Mike Torrez pitching to Graig Nettles
(He pops up to shortstop.)
Fourth inning, one out, one base runner
Red Sox lead 1–0

Telly, Cary, and Frank

All right,
A big hubbub right in back of the Yankee dugout,
Dead center,
Telly Savalas!
We might have to ask him to put a hat on his head,
It's shining up here,
Some glare,
But that's the thing lately,
They say being bald is very sexy,
All right,
I tell ya,
Just about everybody you want to name
Will be here tonight.
Cary Grant hasn't missed a game
Here at Yankee Stadium at the playoffs.
Frank Sinatra has been here.
And we're ready.

October 14, 1976
AMERICAN LEAGUE EAST PLAYOFF
Final game
Kansas City at New York
Ed Figueroa pitching to Al Cowens
First inning, no outs, bases empty
No score

Phil Rizzuto

They Own the Wind

i tell ya,
did you take notice of the flag?
i couldn't believe it.
just as jim rice came to the plate,
the wind started blowing to left field.
it not only helped yastrzemski's homer,
but it hurt jackson's,
the wind was blowing to right field
when jackson hit the fly ball,
when yaz hit the homer
the wind was blowing to left field,
kept it from going foul.
strike one to piniella.
somebody told me
the red sox control the elements up here
i didn't believe 'em until today

October 2, 1978
AMERICAN LEAGUE EAST PLAYOFF
New York at Boston
Mike Torrez pitching to Lou Piniella
Third inning, no outs, bases empty
Red Sox lead 1—0

Prayer for the Captain

There's a little prayer I always say
Whenever I think of my family or when I'm flying,
When I'm afraid, and I am afraid of flying.
It's just a little one. You can say it no matter what,
Whether you're Catholic or Jewish or Protestant
    or whatever.
And I've probably said it a thousand times
Since I heard the news on Thurman Munson.

It's not trying to be maudlin or anything.
His Eminence, Cardinal Cooke, is going to come out
And say a little prayer for Thurman Munson.
But this is just a little one I say time and time again,
It's just: *Angel of God, Thurman's guardian dear,*
To whom his love commits him here there or everywhere,
Ever this night and day be at his side,
To light and guard, to rule and guide.

For some reason it makes me feel like I'm talking to
    Thurman,
Or whoever's name you put in there,
Whether it be my wife or any of my children, my parents
    or anything.
It's just something to keep you really from going bananas.
Because if you let this,
If you keep thinking about what happened, and you can't
    understand it,

Phil Rizzuto

That's what really drives you to despair.

Faith. You gotta have faith.
You know, they say time heals all wounds,
And I don't quite agree with that a hundred percent.
It gets you to cope with wounds.
You carry them the rest of your life.

August 3, 1979
Baltimore at New York
Pre-game show

The Man in the Moon

The Yankees have had a traumatic four days.
Actually five days.
That terrible crash with Thurman Munson.
To go through all that agony,
And then today,
You and I along with the rest of the team
Flew to Canton for the services,
And the family . . .
   Very upset.

You know, it might,
It might sound a little corny.
But we have the most beautiful full moon tonight.
And the crowd,
Enjoying whatever is going on right now.
They say it might sound corny,
But to me it's some kind of a,
   Like an omen.

Both the moon and Thurman Munson,
Both ascending up into heaven.
I just can't get it out of my mind.
I just saw that full moon,
And it just reminded me of Thurman.
   And that's it.

Phil Rizzuto

August 6, 1979
Baltimore at New York
Ron Guidry pitching to Lee May
Fifth inning, bases empty, no outs
Orioles lead 1–0

The Bridge

Two balls and a strike.
You know what they had on TV today, White?
Bridge on the River Kwai.
Everybody should have gotten an Academy Award for that
  movie.
I don't know how many times I've seen it.
About forty times.
Alec Guinness!
William Holden!
Three and one the count.
I just heard somebody whistle.
You know that song?
That's what they whistle.
Nobody out.
And he pops it up.

> May 5, 1987
> New York at Chicago
> Joe Niekro pitching to Carlton Fisk
> Second inning, no outs, bases empy
> No score

Phil Rizzuto

Poem for The Last Picture Show

Wait a minute, that's right!
He's from this little town.
And the cars, he said.
They ride up and down on Main Street all night.
And they never get out of their cars.
And that's the way it was in that movie.
With those old model, old . . .
O, that was really really an excellent picture.

>   July 29, 1991
>   Oakland at New York
>   Jeff Johnson pitching to Willie Wilson
>   First inning, one out, bases empty
>   No score

Never Say Never

Never!
That—
NEVER!
I shouldn't say "Never."
Even James Bond said
"Never say never."
That was a hit.
Right?

> June 27, 1991
> New York at Boston
> Tom Bolton pitching to Randy Velarde
> Third inning, two outs, one base runner
> Yankees lead 4–0

Vincent

O wait a minute.
You gotta take one shot of this.
'Cause this is a true . . .
This is,
This is true.
I was,
Say . . .
That?
HEY THAT'S VINCENT GARDENIA!
HEY!
O he was in *Death Wish*.
With Charles Bronson.
He was mean.
And he really got shot up.
Holy Cow.

>   August 9, 1992
>   Boston at New York
>   Sam Militello pitching to Jack Clark
>   Second inning, no outs, bases empty
>   Yankees lead 3–0

To Cut the "H"

Ever see that movie,
My Cousin Vinnie?
Joe Pesci?

In this movie,
My Cousin Vinnie,
He's talking to the judge.

And he says,
"Those yoots,"
And the judge says,

"What's a yoot?"
A yoot.
And it is a *youth*.

In Brooklyn,
A lot of times,
You cut out the "h."

You use the "t."
You know?

      August 28, 1992
      New York at Minnesota
      Scott Erickson pitching to Roberto Kelly
      Sixth inning, no outs, bases empty
      Twins lead 1–0

Phil Rizzuto

I Never Cried

You know where that came from?
That saying?
Murcer?
That movie,
A League of Their Own.
With the gals.
Tom Hanks is a manager.
And he's a riot.
He's drunk all the time
At the beginning.
And then he turns out to,
One girl cries,
Because she didn't get a hit
Or something.
And he screams,
"There's no crying in baseball."

> August 15, 1992
> New York at Chicago
> Charlie Hough pitching to Bernie Williams
> Third inning, one out, bases empty
> No score

I Walk with Fear

Boy
I never forget
The first Dracula movie
I ever saw.
BELA LUGOSI!

> June 27, 1991
> New York at Boston
> Tom Bolton pitching to Roberto Kelly
> Third inning, no outs, bases empty
> Yankees lead 2—0

Phil Rizzuto

The Question of White's Whereabouts

That was a weird play!
Wait a minute!
That hit the bat twice!
That should be a foul ball!
Here comes Piniella out!
That hit the bat twice!
Now he's saying he's off the bag!
Son of a gun!
I can't believe that!
Let's look at this!
Look at that!
That ball came up and hit the bat!
Twice!
White, where were you when we needed you?

May 2, 1987
Minnesota at New York
Juan Berenguer pitching to Willie Randolph
(Ground ball to the pitcher)
Seventh inning, two outs, bases empty
Yankees lead 5–2

White's Secret

You know what I did?
I forgot
I don't like your line-up card, White.
I like mine better.
But unfortunately
I left mine at home.
I did not bring today's line-up card.

So I borrowed one from Bill White.
He's the professional type.
You know, Martin?
He's got all . . .
I can't figure half the stuff on this card.
Why you need it.
But he does his homework.
He does it well.

But anyway,
Oh yeah.
He's got the highlights.
He's on the ball.
But where Kunkel's name is ninth,
I put the strikeout by Brower.
Oh, he jammed him.

Phil Rizzuto

Foul back.
What happened?

> May 13, 1987
> New York at Texas
> Dennis Rasmussen pitching to Bob Brower
> Third inning, two out, bases empty
> Yankees lead 3–0

Forever Young

Bobby Thigpen out there.
Number thirty-seven.
That's the guy in the *Peanuts* cartoon.
Pigpen.
That's a joke.
That guy in *Peanuts* with Charlie Brown.
He's always dirty.
Oh yeah.
Every day.
Orphan Annie.
You know,
She hasn't aged in thirty-two years.

> May 12, 1987
> Chicago at New York
> Bill Long pitching to Don Mattingly
> Sixth inning, no outs, one base runner
> Yankees lead 3–1

The Penguin

O THAT'S GONE!
HOLY COW!
WATCH THE—
Look at the Penguin!
It's not gone.

I was watching him run.
Wait a minute.
When he hit it
That was the funniest run I've ever seen.
Watch this.

> May 31, 1987
> Oakland at New York
> Tommy John pitching to Ron Cey
> Second inning, no outs, bases empty
> (long fly to left)
> Tie score 1–1

T-Bone

One ball, one strike
Two out, two on
The Yankees trail four to one
In the bottom of the seventh.
Michelle wants to say
"Happy birthday to T-bone."
That's his name: T-Bone.
The runners leading away . . .

> July 26, 1991
> California at New York
> Mark Langston pitching to Bernie Williams
> Game status as indicated.

Phil Rizzuto

To Speak with Espy, to Smile with Tears

I just told him, I said:
"Look,
"You're a professional.
"You've got to stop this squabbling in the papers.
"It's the worst thing you can do.
"Just go out there and play your regular game.
"Show them that you're capable
"Of playing every day."
He smiled for the first time.
I said, "Geh."
(Now you won't believe this.)
I said, "GET THREE FOR THREE!"
I know . . .
It sounds like I made it up.
I really did make it up.
It's such a lousy game
That I gotta make up something.

> April 12, 1991
> New York at Kansas City
> Storm Davis pitching to Steve Sax
> Seventh inning, no outs, one base runner
> (Following Alvaro Espinoza's third hit)
> Royals lead 8–4

Message to the Doctor

How'd you make out?
With Doctor Bonetti?
What?
I was talking to Bobby Murcer that time.
Thought I had the mike off.
He wants to play golf tomorrow.
So if Doctor Bonetti is listening,
He can give him a call
For Murcer is very anxious
To play golf.
Where?
High fly.
And Kelly's got it.

June 9, 1992
Toronto at New York
Tim Leary pitching to Jeff Kent
Sixth inning, one out, bases empty
Score tied 1–1

Phil Rizzuto

Spirit of '76

I don't mean
To spoil all your fun, Murcer.
But this guy goes to a golf course
That I have been playing since
It was built.
Have trouble on it.
He never saw the course.
Bobby Murcer!
He was my partner.
And shot a seventy-six.
SEVENTY-SIX!

> August 30, 1992
> New York at Minnesota
> Kevin Tapani pitching to Randy Velarde
> Fourth inning, two outs, bases empty
> Twins lead 1—0

The Way Mattingly Wants Them to Do

Down in Florida, I'm telling you
They're rooting so hard,
They count, they say:
"We gotta win some games!"
And to see something like this,
You know, with the fans,
The ballplayers getting excited
The way Mattingly wants them to do,
Instead of laying back
And waiting to get beat,
The way so many ball clubs used to do
Against the Yankees,
You know, they used to say,
"Some way they're going to beat us."
And they do.

    May 10, 1991
    Oakland at New York
    Greg Cadaret pitching to Willie Wilson
    Eighth inning, no outs, bases empty
    Yankees lead 5–3

Phil Rizzuto

Challenge to Youth

I tell you what I would change:
That NO BALK to second base.
You know,
You can do anything to second base.
Yeah, I never did like that.
What would you change?

> May 10, 1991
> Oakland at New York
> John Habyan pitching to Mark McGwire
> Seventh inning, one out, one base runner
> Orioles lead 3–2

Martin's Rules

They should have different ways
Of determining the pennant winner, Martin.
Like you do in golf, you know?

You say, "All right,
"I'll give you two strokes on the front side
"And one on the back side."
So they take all the standings
Of east and west together,
And they break them up in half.

Then you've got a chance of winning one.

May 1, 1987
New York at Minnesota
Rick Rhoden pitching to Gary Gaetti
First inning, no outs, one base runner
Twins lead 1—0

Phil Rizzuto

O Mickey

Our buddy Mickey Mantle,
You know what a prankster he is.
So I get a phone call.
I'm watching
The Bridge on the River Kwai.

I'm very intense when I watch a movie.
Because I try . . .
I've seen the movie so many times
I can go along,
Lip-synch with it.

So Mick gets on the phone.
"Hey Mick . . . how ya—?"
"Ooo, I'm terrible.
"I had another heart attack,
"And the doctor says I can't live."

I say, "Oooo, MICK!"
He says, "Yeah . . ."
But before I go,
"I want to interview you."
I could've shot him.

I had to take a pill.

May 5, 1987
New York at Chicago
Bill Long pitching to Joel Skinner
Third inning, no outs, bases empty
No score

Phil Rizzuto

Champion

Remember that fellow I told you.
Champ Marble?
Champ Marble.
He's a hundred and two years old.
When he was a hundred years old, I told you.
Last year he was a hundred and one.
This year he is a hundred and two.
Played golf with him over at Upper Montclair Country Club.
He's probably in bed now.
A little low.
One ball, two strikes.
His name is Champ Marble.
James F. Marble to be exact.
I mean really a tremendous man.
He doesn't wear glasses.
No hearing aid.
Sees better than me.
Hits better than me.
Better than me.
High and tight.
Two and two.

April 12, 1991
New York at Kansas City
Chuck Cary pitching to Gary Thurman
Third inning, two outs, two base runners
Score tied 3—3

Way Up Here

I can see now, way up here,
Why a lot of the official scorers
Maybe think that hard-hit balls
Might be errors, you know.
You get a different conception.

September 25, 1960
Boston at New York
Mike Fornieles pitching to Gil McDougald
Ninth inning, bases empty, no outs
Yankees lead 4–2
Final: Yankees 4, Red Sox 3

Phil Rizzuto

Giliad

I was with Gil McDougald the other day.
Oh boy.
He looks great.
Playing golf over in Spring Lakes Golf Club.
Sad thing is that,
You know,
He's totally deaf now.
FOUL! He stays alive!
Still got a great sense of humor.
But he had to retire,
Because he was getting all those phone calls
In his business.
And he just couldn't,
No way could he hear anything.
So he sold his business.
Very happy.
They love him down there at Spring Lake.

But I was very happy.
'Cause he does talk and tell stories and,
He's not a good listener,
But one thing he told me
That I was very happy about—
LOW! BALL FOUR!
WHAT AN EYE BY NOKES!
How do you like that?
Behind 0 and 2 and he works his way for a walk!
You know what McDougald told me when he saw me?

O Holy Cow!

41

He hadn't seen me for a while.
He said, "I wanna tell you something.
"You're not as ugly as you look on TV."
He said to me.
I said, "Thanks Gil."

> May 25, 1991
> New York at Baltimore
> Mike Flanagan pitching to Matt Nokes
> Ninth inning, no outs, bases empty
> Score tied 4–4

Phil Rizzuto

Kubek and Trautwig and Phillips or Powers

Tony is having a little problem
With his uh—oh yeah, Traut,
I want to tell you something about Trautwig.
He had the greatest interview that I have ever heard.
With Richie Phillips the basketball umpire.
Referee.
I gotta get him over here.
Holy.

Can I, uh, can we give?
Give him the microphone
Just to talk about this?

Look at Kubek over there.
Kubek's voice is going.
I might have to stick around
But Al Trautwig is here
And I heard an interview
I couldn't believe it
With Richie Phillips . . .
Richie Powers.
I just want to tell you
I just couldn't believe it.
Kubek over there.

I tell you.
I couldn't believe what I was hearing.
About Richie Powers

O Holy Cow!

When he said to you,
"The last thing I think about before I go to sleep,
"Is this the night I'm gonna commit suicide?"
Am I right?
I tell you,
This was really great.

> August 11, 1991
> Detroit at New York
> Paul Gibson pitching to Pat Kelly
> Sixth inning, no outs, bases empty
> Yankees lead 8–6.

Phil Rizzuto

Dickie Poem Number One

Dickie Thon the batter.
Now way way back when he first came
Into the big leagues,
I mention the fact that I used to play
With his grandfather.
Baseball.
Sandlot baseball.
He went away to the minor leagues.
And during the service time,
He was in Puerto Rico.
And he was a very
Astute young man.
Don't forget,
This was way back
In the Second World War.
Grounder to short,
And Velarde just flips
To Stankiewicz for the force.
And that'll do it.
And I'll finish my story later.

April 27, 1992
Texas at New York
Scott Sanderson pitching to Dickie Thon
Fourth inning, two outs, one base runner
Yankees lead 3–1

Dickie Poem Number Two

Wait!
I never finished
This story about Dickie Thon!
I told you I played ball
With his grandfather.
And,
And he was so on the ball.
When he went to Puerto Rico
He realized they didn't
Have washing machines.
Things we had in the States.
Ahhhhhhhhhhhh . . .
The son of a gun!
Hit the grounder.
I'll have to finish the story
Next homestand.
Three up.
Three down.

April 27, 1992
Texas at New York
Lee Guetterman pitching to Dickie Thon
Sixth inning, two outs, bases empty
Yankees lead 6–3

Phil Rizzuto

To Murcer, an Explanation

I tried to ask Andy Stankiewicz.
He won't say anything though,
Why he's not playing a little more.
And I said, "Are you hurt?"
He said, "No. I'm not hurt.
"Feel great."

Of course,
He never does complain, Murcer.
But I figured I was talking to myself there
A little while,
And it was very uninteresting.
That's why I brought you in.

> September 1, 1992
> New York at Milwaukee
> Jamie Navarro pitching to Bernie Williams
> First inning, no outs, bases empty
> No score

1961 and 1991

Oh man,
You talk about having fun broadcasting games.
That year, I mean, there were home runs every day.
There was nothing but a lot of runs.
Makes it a lot easier.
All right!
Here's Lovullo.
Torey Lovullo.
I've been calling him "Tony."
And he pops it up.

> April 13, 1991
> New York at Kansas City
> Bret Saberhagen pitching to Torey Lovullo
> Third inning, no outs, bases empty
> Royals lead 2–0

Phil Rizzuto

Remember When

O it was always intense.
Just as you said
And it was not a regular
Not a regular game at all.
It was every game meant so much,
You know,
One seemed to top the other.

> May 28, 1991
> Boston at New York
> Roger Clemens pitching to Hensley Meulens
> Fifth inning, no outs, bases empty
> Boston leads 4–1

On Having to Go to Kansas City

That's going to ruin the rest,
The rest of the year,
For me now.
O, no.
I mean,
Thinking of that long trip
For one, one game.
To say sayonara and good-bye.
It's not that I don't want to be doing it.
It's . . . come on,
Get me out of this, Seaver.
Come on.
You're doing nothing back there.

> August 28, 1992
> New York at Minnesota
> Scott Sanderson pitching to Brian Harper
> Second inning, no outs, bases empty
> Twins lead 1–0

Phil Rizzuto

My Only Friend, the End

I.

And here comes Casey Stengel.
And I believe he's gonna call in the man
Who has been his insurance the last half of this season,
Louie Arroyo!
With the left-handed hitter up there,
Casey will probably bring in Arroyo,
And that's the sign he makes,
For the left-hander.
Terry is out of there.

II.

Louie Arroyo coming on,
Will be trying to get rid of Pete Runnels,
If he possibly can,
And he's got himself a tough job,
As Jackie Jensen just told you,
Pete Runnels is the type hitter
Who does not worry
About whether it's a left-hander or right-hander
Out on the mound,
He as we all know can hit the ball
As hard to left field as he does to right field.
It's gonna be a battle now,
Pete just trying to meet the ball,
And Arroyo trying to outguess him on the hill.

III.

Pete Runnels the batter,
Runners at first and third,
The Yankees lead four to three
We're in the bottom of the ninth inning,
Arroyo into the stretch position.
The pitch is POPPED FOUL
AND BOBBY RICHARDSON IS UNDER IT
AND MAKES THE CATCH,
AND THE YANKEES WIN THE PENNANT,
THE TWENTY-FIFTH PENNANT
IN THE YANKEES' CAREER.

>   September 25, 1960
>   Boston at New York
>   Luis Arroyo pitching to Pete Runnels
>   Ninth inning, two base runners, two out
>   Yankees lead 4–3

Phil Rizzuto

Poem No. 61

Here comes Roger Maris.
They're standing up.
Waiting to see if Roger
Is going to hit
Number sixty-one.
Here's the windup.
The pitch to Roger.
Way outside.
Ball one.

The fans are starting to boo.
Low . . .
Ball two.
That one was in the dirt.
And the boos get louder.
Two balls, no strikes
On Roger Maris . . .

Here's the windup.
Fastball
HIT DEEP TO RIGHT—
THIS COULD BE IT.
WAY BACK THERE.
HOLY COW.
HE DID IT.

SIXTY-ONE HOME RUNS.
They're fighting for the ball out there.

> October 1, 1961 WPIX–TV
> Boston at New York
> Roger Maris batting against Tracy Stallard
> Fourth inning, no score, bases empty
> Final: Yankees 1, Red Sox 0

Phil Rizzuto

A Life for Mickey

The pitch to Mick: A swing and a miss,
And, boy, he was going for the downs on that one.
Two balls, two strikes.
Sun shining brightly here today.
This is the best day we've had
Of the three days we've played ball here in Detroit.
All right, ready for the two-two delivery.
Wilson's pitch—is foul tipped,
And in and out of the glove of Freehan,
A life for Mickey.
And now Mick goes back,
Wants the pine tar rag, a little better grip.
Pepitone hands it to him. Two and two.
The scoreboard thought it was strike three.
Now they put the count up there again.
Two and two, one man out.
Earl Wilson ready to pitch to Mantle.
He kicks, delivers: it's high and outside,
Ball three, three and two,
Freehan gives the sign.
Wilson ready for the payoff pitch.
Here is is: And it's hit deep to right,
THAT'S GONE! WAY BACK UP THERE!
Two-run homer for Mantle,
Who has now homered in four consecutive ball games.

And suddenly it's a seven to four ball game.
Mickey Mantle really stroking that potato!

> May 21, 1967
> New York at Detroit
> Earl Wilson pitching to Mickey Mantle
> Seventh inning, one base runner, one out
> Tigers lead 7—4

Phil Rizzuto

Ellie's Shot

So it's two away,
And here's Elston Howard,
Leading both leagues in hitting.
Two out, nobody on, no score.
Top of the second.
The Yankees and the White Sox.
From Comiskey Park in Chicago.
Now the two-one pitch.

THERE'S A DRIVE DEEP TO LEFT FIELD!
THAT BALL IS GONE!
WAY BACK!
TREMENDOUS HOME RUN!
MAN!
ELLIE REALLY TAGGED THAT ONE!
WHAT A SHOT THAT WAS!

> July 14, 1961
> New York at Chicago
> Ray Herbert pitching to Elston Howard
> Game situation as stated.

Confrontation

Ted Williams made this remark now.
And I'm not saying it
Because I agree with him wholeheartedly.
But he said,
"Pitchers are the dumbest ballplayers of all ballplayers.
"Infielders, outfielders," he says.
"'Cause all they know how to do is pitch.
"And they only pitch one out of every five days."
Now I'm just saying,
What?
What did you think of that statement?
Bouncer.
And Sax to his left.
Throws him out.
One away.
I'm asking you a simple question, Seaver.
There he is.
He won't answer me.
How do you like my shirt?
You see my shirt?
Rocky Marciano.

> July 23, 1991
> Seattle at New York
> Scott Kamieniecki pitching to Greg Briley
> Seventh inning, no outs, bases empty
> Mariners lead 2—1

Phil Rizzuto

To Murcer, on a Storm Long Ago

You were playing and I was broadcasting.
We were on the field.
And all of a sudden
One of those claps of thunder
That only happens here in Kansas City and Oklahoma
And lightning
And I took off.

And Bobby was professional enough.
I'd just asked him a question.
I forgot what that was.
But he answered the question and said:
"We'll be right back after this."
He came back, but I was gone.
Oooo, man.

> April 13, 1991
> New York at Kansas City
> Tim Leary pitching to Danny Tartabull
> Third inning, one out, bases empty
> Royals lead 2–1

Abandoned in a Storm

Whoa!
I wasn't even looking at the sky
And I saw that!
I'm sorry, man.
I cannot handle this.
Low, ball one.

Livingstone the batter.
He's flied to center
And doubled to left.
Where are you going?
Murcer!
Get ba—

Get back here!
One ball and no strikes.
Outside.
Two and nothing.
Two men out.
If this was a g—

Wait!
Wait!
Seaver!
Come back!
If this was a g—
And Moore!

Phil Rizzuto

Where?
Where is everybody?
Listen!
If this was a golf tournament,
Everybody'd leave.
But you got . . .

Come on!
O, got'm!
No!
Safe!
Come on!
You got me talking to myself.

> August 10, 1992
> New York at Detroit
> Jerry Nielsen pitching to Scott Livingstone
> Fifth inning, two outs, one base runner
> Tigers lead 5–3

DiMaggio's Bat

I started to tell you this story
And I was rudely interrupted by somebody.
Not Seaver though.
I want to make that clear . . .
Today,
When I went to get the newspaper,
This gentleman,
His name is Phil,
Same as mine,
Brought in a bat.
I thought he was going to give it to me.
Joe DiMaggio's bat.
And it had "US ARMY" on it.
DiMag was in the army.
He got it in Hawaii.
His brother,
This Phil's brother,
Was stationed with DiMaggio.
And DiMaggio gave him a bat.
And you should see that thing.
And he wanted to know if it was worth money.
I said, "It's worth a lot of money.
"And if we can get DiMaggio's name on it,
"It'll be worth ten times more."
The wood . . .
I mean,
You couldn't chip that bat.
That's the way DiMaggio's wood was on the bats.

Phil Rizzuto

He would ask for that type of wood.
Being an old fisherman
He knew about the trees.

June 5, 1992
Detroit at New York
Scott Sanderson pitching to Lou Whitaker
Fourth inning, two outs, two base runners
Tigers lead 4–1

O What a Huddle Out There

I.

Now I had started to tell you
When I saw Billy Martin make the motion
For Gossage to come on
That it brings back some nightmares.
When George Brett in 1980,
The year the Royals beat the Yankees in the playoffs,
Right here at Yankee Stadium,
Hit a 95-mile-an-hour fastball thrown by the Gossage
A hundred twenty miles an hour into the upper deck
Here at Yankee stadium.
And the best fastball pitcher in baseball
And just about the best fastball hitter in baseball,
George Brett,
What a confrontation.

The set, the pitch,
AND A DRIVE TO DEEP LEFT FIELD
And curving foul . . .
Holy cow.
Where's Bill White?
Bill White is in his car on the way home,
Not up here getting nervous and cold.
Long strike.

The set by Gossage, the pitch,
DEEP TO RIGHT FIELD

Phil Rizzuto

HOLY COW I DON'T BELIEVE IT!
HOME RUN FOR GEORGE BRETT!
I don't believe it,
That lightning could strike twice,
And Billy Martin now is coming out,
He wants to take a look at that bat,
But it's a little late.
I don't believe it.
I told you I have nightmares about this man.
Unbelievable!

Hey, they might have a point here!
Thurman Munson was called out after getting a base hit
Because there was pine tar above—
You can see the bat!
Well no you can't because we're not on TV,
Above the trademark!
And Billy Martin might have a valid point here!
That's the only way the Yankees can get out of this scrape.

Holy Cow, I can't believe it.
Brett hit that ball nine miles.
Billy pointing to the bat!
Now Thurman Munson had gotten a base hit out in
    Minnesota.
And the manager of the Twins at that time
Asked the umpire to look at the bat,
And they called Thurman Munson out,
And Martin has a very valid argument here.
And if he wins this,
There will be chaos.

O Holy Cow!

Look at George Brett.
He's getting congratulated.
But there's a big huddle out there.
And the umpires, they've got to talk,
To get a calibrating machine out here
And calibrate this thing
And see just how high the pine tar is,
And there is a definite rule in the rule book
That you cannot have it above a certain distance!

O what a huddle out there.
They're really . . .
Billy Martin standing with his arms folded out there.
Boy, he was quickly off that bench.
WELL LOOK WHO HAS RETURNED!
He made a U-turn on the bridge!
BILL WHITE IS BACK!
And they are about to make a decision
And this could be a momentous decision.
I can't tell by the way they're walking
Who's going to win this argument.

HE'S OUT!

II.
Well, I tell ya,
There's a rule,
A definite rule in the rule book
That the pine tar can only be a certain height,
And now they're trying to get rid of the bat,
And Gaylord Perry was out there,

He's gonna get fined,
He's in a tug of war with the umpire.

Dick Howser is furious.
They're holding George Brett out there,
Three men are holding him.
He is called out,
And the Yankees win the game four to three,
But it is one of the most unbelievable endings
I have ever seen.

> July 24, 1983 (The Pine Tar Game)
> Kansas City at New York
> Rich Gossage pitching to George Brett
> Ninth inning, one base runner, two outs.
> Yankees lead 4–3
> Brett's home run was later reinstated by the
> Commissioner of Baseball

I Really Should Be Going Home

It's very chilly.
As a matter—
I'm telling you,
I've been freezing.
My hands are cold.
I have low blood pressure anyway.
And arthritis.
I really should be going home.

> July 24, 1983 (The Pine Tar Game)
> Kansas City at New York
> Mike Armstrong pitching to Rick Cerone
> Seventh inning, bases empty, two outs.
> Yankees lead 4–3

Phil Rizzuto

Toying with Seaver, Soaring with Utica

Utica, New York!
There's a cow up there.
That won its 300th game.
And stepped on my foot that day . . .
And he had a calf.
And they're both up there
On a farm in Utica.
And I went . . .

I tried to borrow a gun
To shoot the cow.
'Course it would happen to be a day
That some guy won his 300th game . . .

He'd never let me forget it.
They wanted,
The mayor wanted to have a parade.
With me and the two cows . . .

I said, "Forget it."

> April 27, 1992
> Texas at New York
> Scott Sanderson pitching to Kevin Reimer
> Fifth inning, two outs, one base runner
> Tie score 3–3

When Your Eyes Start Bouncing

That was a riot.
'Cause Velarde was gonna try and ca—
Watch this:

Now he runs by Velarde.
Velarde says:
"What's coming off here?"

And that's tough when
You're running hard
And your eyes start bouncing.

> May 17, 1992
> Oakland at New York
> Shawn Hillegas pitching to Mark McGwire
> Ninth inning, one out, one base runner
> Pop fly to second base
> A's lead 6—3

Phil Rizzuto

That Voice

Moore is talking to me.
In the other ear.
Heh?
Confusing me.

July 9, 1992
Seattle at New York
Scott Kamieniecki pitching to Jay Buhner
Fourth inning, one out, bases empty
Yankees lead 7–3

The Thirty Rank

Today is John Moore's birthday.
And he's a little nervous.
He left the twenty rank,

And he's in the thirty rank now.
A lot of people
Can't handle that.

> July 9, 1992
> Seattle at New York
> Scott Kamieniecki pitching to Jay Buhner
> Fourth inning, one out, bases empty
> Yankees lead 7–3

Phil Rizzuto

No Nokes

Nokes?
Didn't you tell me
Nokes is going to be an All Star?
No?
Must've been Seaver then.

> June 28, 1991
> New York at Milwaukee
> Don August pitching to Matt Nokes
> Third inning, no outs, bases empty
> Yankees lead 2–0

Caps, Bees, Jokes, Pags

Today is Cap Day.
Today is Cap Day.

We have talked about the bees
That we had showed on camera

Out in Cincinnati.
I was just joking,

But my jokes are pretty sick
I've been told by certain people.

He didn't get it.
And Pags, a high fly to center field.

> May 10, 1987
> Minnesota at New York
> Joe Klink pitching to Mike Pagliarulo
> Third inning, two outs, bases empty
> Yankees lead 4–0

Phil Rizzuto

No Pain

I tell ya,
There's a great group down in Suite 332.
Or is it 328?
I think it's 328.
Oh . . .

All the doctors from St. Barnabas Hospital
Where I was operated on.
And they did an excellent job.
I told them I didn't like the sight of blood.
So they knocked me out.

Of the sort.
I didn't like pain.
I had no pain.
Unbelievable.
I'm not kidding you.

> June 5, 1992
> Detroit at New York
> Frank Tanana pitching to Pat Kelly
> Fourth inning, one out, two base runners
> Tigers lead 4–1

Question to Moore

Hey Moore,
Can I talk about
The no-hitter now?

No?
Okay.
I won't.

> July 9, 1992
> Seattle at New York
> Scott Kamieniecki pitching to Omar Vizquel
> Fifth inning, one out, bases empty
> Yankees lead 7–3

Phil Rizzuto

None of My Business

Everybody has
Their own things to iron out.
You have reasons for doing things.

I'm not going to ask you about that.
But I mean . . .
You look in great shape!

> September 25, 1960
> Boston at New York
> Ralph Terry pitching to Pumpsie Green
> (Speaking to retired Red Sox Jackie Jensen)
> Ninth inning, one base runner, one out
> Yankees lead 4–2

Clarification

I think it's 'cause Murcer talks slow,
'Cause he's from Oklahoma,
This game is going so slow.
No?

September 4, 1992
Texas at New York
Rich Monteleone pitching to Monty Fariss
Sixth inning, one out, bases loaded
Yankees lead 6–3

Phil Rizzuto

Why I Do What I Do

Well, I'll tell ya,
Once you finish playing ball,
You gotta find other ways
To make a living.
Especially
When you got four children.

September 25, 1960
Boston at New York
Mike Fornieles pitching to Dale Long
Ninth inning, bases empty, no outs
Yankees lead 4–2

Haiku

Ice, I can't stand it.
I cannot stand anything
Cold on my body.

> May 31, 1991
> Milwaukee at New York
> Julio Machado pitching to Hensley Meulens
> Eighth inning, no outs, bases empty
> Score tied 2–2

Phil Rizzuto

Joe R.

Anyway . . .
Joe Rossomando
He was a good player.
I mean,
He looked a lot like Joe DiMaggio.
I'm tellin' ya,
He had a terrible collision at home plate.
In the minor leagues
And almost,
Almost swallowed his tongue
If it hadn't been
Uh,
For the trainer,
Came out,
Put a piece of wood in there.
Or something there.
Ohhh,
I couldn't look,
But he was an excellent player.
But anyway . . .
He's still coaching at Yale.
Just as old as I am.
He stays in great shape.
With his wife Marylou
And his daughter,
Mary Beth.
Who has graduated from Yale,
And has gone back

To take her master's there.
That's enough.

August 19, 1991, WPIX-TV
Kansas City at New York
Mike Boddicker pitching to Matt Nokes
Eighth inning, one out, one base runner
Score tied 2–2
Final: Yankees 6, Royals 2

Phil Rizzuto

Who?

Did you hit me, Seaver?
Somebody hit me.
STRUCK'M OUT!

> July 6, 1992
> Minnesota at New York
> Carl Willis pitching to Pat Kelly
> Sixth inning, bases empty, two outs
> Twins lead 10–5

Poem for Jesse

Heyyyyyyyyy!
That's it!
Holy cow!
He did it!
Holy cow!
Look at Jesse Barfield!
I wanna tell you!
Ho ho ho ho!
Whoooooooooooooooah!
You got it, Murcer!
My heart.
My heart won't take it anymore.
I'm tellin' ya,
Holy cow!
I mean,
That is an unbelievable finish!
Are we on the air?
We're on the air?
We're on the?
Hooooooooooooooah.
Wow!
This Yankee Club is something!
I tell ya!
Atta boy, Jesse!

Phil Rizzuto

May 31, 1991
Milwaukee at New York
Chuck Crim pitching to Jesse Barfield
(Game-winning home run)
Ninth inning, two outs, bases empty
Yankees win 3—2

I Hate Myself

Ooooo!
THAT'S GONNA BE
UP THE ALLEY
FOR EXTRA BASES!
Noooo!
WHY DON'T I SHUT UP!
Noooo.
Nokes thought
The same thing I did.
An easy double—
I can't believe it.
Holy cow.
Put my foot in my mouth right there.

Double play.

> June 20, 1992
> New York at Baltimore
> Alan Mills pitching to Charlie Hayes
> Seventh inning, two out, one base runner
> Fly to right, Matt Nokes doubled off first
> Orioles lead 10–7

O, I Love to Watch Those Wrestlers!

O I love to watch those wrestlers!
I used to know
All the old-time wrestlers.
They were great, I mean.

It's a great sport,
A lot of people,
You know, they think it's all fixed.
Lined deep to right.

> June 15, 1992
> New York at Boston
> Scott Sanderson pitching to Tony Pena
> Third inning, no outs, bases empty
> No score

Incident in an Elevator

I.

Hey Brew,
What was that wrestler's name
That we met on the way out?
Jimmy Snuka we met.
Just as we were saying good-bye
To the governor of your fine state
Of Oklahoma.

II.

Yes,
A real young-looking governor,
I'll tell you that.
And this wrestler came by.
I mean, he scared me.
He had a camouflage outfit on
With this camouflage thing on his head.
Big bruiser.

III.

No,
It wasn't Sergeant Slaughter.
This guy had a better tan
Than Sergeant Slaughter ever had.
And he, I mean,
He came in and Brew,
Brew went crazy.

Phil Rizzuto

"There's Jimmy Snuka!
"He put five state troopers,
"Knocked 'em out!"
That's a true story.

      September 15, 1992
      Chicago at New York
      Russ Springer pitching to Ron Karkovice
      Ninth inning, no outs, bases empty
      White Sox lead 4–2

Laughter Behind the Tears

Peterson delivers.
A foul off Josephson's foot.
And back to the on-deck circle.
And Josephson limping
Around home plate.
One and one.

He's still walking around,
Trying to get a little feeling
Back in that left foot.
Josephson has twenty-six
Runs batted in for the Red Sox.
A right-handed batter.

Peterson winds.
The pitch is . . .
Fouled off his foot again!
Two in a row.
Heh heh.
He fouled off his left foot.
Heh heh.
It's really nothing to laugh about.

> July 11, 1971
> Boston at New York
> Fritz Peterson pitching to Duane Josephson
> Fifth inning, two base runners, no outs.
> Yankees lead 1—0

Phil Rizzuto

Clete Does Eat

When you're frustrated,
You eat a lot.

And when you're in love,
You eat a lot.

And when you're hungry,
You eat a lot.

So Boyer's doing all three.
That's a little inside joke.

>   August 9, 1992
>   Boston at New York
>   Joe Hesketh pitching to Andy Stankiewicz
>   Second inning, no outs, one base runner
>   Yankees lead 3–0

Squirrels

I.

In the backyard we got a lot of trees.
In our home I've watched them leap
From limb to limb.
Unbelievable.

II.

Did you ever get one in your attic?
They're not too cute
When they get in your attic.
I'll tell you that.

III.

I would not harm a squirrel.
I don't want to get those animal lovers . . .
I got them in my attic.
No, I got,
But I got a squirrel cage
And trapped them in the cage
Then took them out in the woods
Over by Yogi's house
And dropped them off.

June 7, 1991
Texas at New York
John Habyan pitching to Steve Buchelle
Ninth inning, one out, bases empty
Tie score 4–4

Phil Rizzuto

Buns

He has powerful legs and cute buns,
That Henderson.
That was a great shot,
Going to second base there.
There's nothing wrong with that, White.
That's a popular expression.
High, and it's one and one.
His legs were churning.

> May 10, 1987
> New York at Minnesota
> Charlie Hudson pitching to Al Newman
> (Replay of stolen base)
> Third inning, no outs, bases empy
> Yankees lead 4–0

Legs

The legs are so important.
In golf they're very,
People don't realize
How important legs are in golf,
Or in baseball,
And football, definitely.
Track.
O, in track.
All-important.
Jumping.
Soccer.
Is there anything, what?
Is there anything where the legs
Are not the most important?

> May 28, 1991
> Boston at New York
> Roger Clemens pitching to Jesse Barfield
> Seventh inning, one out, bases empty
> Boston leads 6–1

Phil Rizzuto

Rocket Love

Mmmmmmmm.
That's a lotta man there.
Got under it.
High pop-up.

> May 28, 1991
> Boston at New York
> Roger Clemens pitching to Mel Hall
> Sixth inning, two outs, one base runner
> (Discussing Roger Clemens)
> Boston leads 6—1

The Locked Door

We mention Buck Showalter.
He and I,
For twenty minutes,
Were trying to find a way
To get into the ballpark.

He was lucky.
He went down the tunnel.
But I couldn't go down there.
They said I didn't have the right credentials.
And I couldn't get in the door
That we got in tonight.

> June 20, 1992
> New York at Baltimore
> Bob Milacki pitching to Mel Hall
> First inning, one out, bases empty
> No score

Phil Rizzuto

On Journalism

You gotta get down to the basic facts
You don't get, what?
Get the story if you want to be a good reporter.
And find out if it is true!
And then I hate it when I read it in the paper
Or TV comes out with a premature
FOUL BALL!
With a premature explanation.
Or whatever it is.

> June 22, 1991
> Minnesota at New York
> Wade Taylor pitching to Gene Larkin
> Sixth inning, two outs, bases empty
> Twins lead 2–0

On Capitalism

We await the end of a long commercial
For the umpires to say,
"Time is in."
Well, that's what pays the freight
For these televised games,
You can't have your cake and eat it.

> October 14, 1976
> Kansas City at New York
> AMERICAN LEAGUE PLAYOFF GAME
> Paul Splittorff pitching to Oscar Gamble
> Second inning, no outs, bases empty
> Royals lead 3–2

Phil Rizzuto

Fatherhood

How about that Rob Wilfong.
Now he wants to quit baseball.
Yeah.
Usually, if a ballplayer gets a taste of family life
And babysitting for the kids,
He wants to go back to playing ball.
But evidently Wilfong likes that.
Never had done that before.
Never had a chance to do it.
High, two and one.

> May 12, 1987
> Chicago at New York
> Joe Niekro pitching to Donnie Hill
> First inning, two outs, two base runners
> White Sox lead 1—0

Boxes

They have more fun with boxes
You know,
When during Christmas
Or any time
You go to buy the kids boxes.
That's what they play with.
You buy them beautiful toys.
They end up playing with the box.

> July 27, 1991
> California at New York
> Greg Cadaret pitching to Dick Schofield
> Fifth inning, no outs, bases empty
> Yankees lead 4–2

Phil Rizzuto

Golden Years

There are mornings
I wake up
And my right leg hurts.

The next morning
My knee hurts.
My shoulder . . .

The golden years
Have slipped by me.
But you gotta hang in there.

A little low.
Two balls
And a strike.

> August 9, 1992
> Boston at New York
> Sam Militello pitching to Jodie Reed
> Third inning, no outs, bases empty
> Yankees lead 3–0

Sisyphus

HEYYYYYYY!
THAT TIES IT UP!
RIGHT THERE!

No.
It doesn't.
O, I'm tellin' ya.

Normally,
When he hits a ball like that,
It's way up in the bleachers.

> July 30, 1991
> Oakland at New York
> Andy Hawkins pitching to Don Mattingly
> (Fly to right)
> Fourth inning, one out, bases empty
> A's lead 2–1

Phil Rizzuto

Gone and Back

OH!
THAT'S GONE!
No.
It's not.

Close.
Off the wall.
Son of a gun.
I make a lot of mistakes like that.

> May 30, 1992
> New York at Milwaukee
> Chris Bosio pitching to Dion James
> Fourth inning, no outs, one base runner
> Double
> Yankees lead 3–0

They're on Reggie

These fans have been
On Reggie all day,
When he went out for outfield practice,
Running around on the field.

He dropped a fly ball
During batting practice,
And they really jumped all over him.
But he can really shut them up now.

Two balls, no strikes on Reggie Jackson.
The pitch by Torrez.
Ooooo, WHAT A CUT!
But he missed it.

> October 2, 1978
> AMERICAN LEAGUE EAST PLAYOFF
> New York at Boston
> Mike Torrez pitching to Reggie Jackson
> (He grounds to second base.)
> Sixth inning, two outs, bases empty
> Red Sox lead 1—0

Phil Rizzuto

Pressure

Tremendous pressure
In this ball game.
You cannot let up a minute

Whether you're pitching.
Catching.
Playing the infield or outfield.

Or coaching.
Or managing.
Or broadcasting.

> October 2, 1978
> AMERICAN LEAGUE EAST PLAYOFF
> New York at Boston
> Ron Guidry pitching to Jack Brohamer
> Fifth inning, two out, one base runner
> Red Sox lead 1–0

On Being in Boston for a One-Game Season

I still can't believe
I'm up here at Fenway Park.

My body feels like
It's in Kansas City,

Waiting for tomorrow's
First playoff game.

> October 2, 1978
> AMERICAN LEAGUE EAST PLAYOFF
> New York at Boston
> Mike Torrez pitching to Lou Piniella
> Third inning, no outs, bases empty
> Red Sox lead 1—0

Phil Rizzuto

Willie

Figueroa swings into the windup
And a bouncer off home plate,
And RANDOLPH'S GONNA HAVE TO HURRY!
He gets it, throws,
HE GOT'M!
Pretty play by Willie Randolph!

And that's one of the toughest plays for any infielder,
A Baltimore Chop off home plate,
Went about thirty feet in the air,
Willie had to get it on the first short hop
And get rid of it in the same motion,
And did!

That youngster is Mister Cool out there.
We gotta give him a big star
On the first play of the ball game.
Willie Randolph! Just a rookie,
But plays like he's been in the big leagues
For ten years!

> October 14, 1976
> AMERICAN LEAGUE EAST PLAYOFF
> Final game
> Kansas City at New York
> Ed Figueroa pitching to Al Cowens
> First inning, no outs, bases empty
> No score

It's Different in the Playoffs

Remember when we were kids
And you threw a pitch you didn't like?
And you'd say, "Oops, slipped!"
And it wouldn't count?
Even if he hit a home run?

Can't work that here.

October 14, 1976
Kansas City at New York
AMERICAN LEAGUE PLAYOFF GAME
Ed Figueroa pitching to John Mayberry
Third inning, no outs, bases empty
Royals lead 3–2

Phil Rizzuto

Q

I used to hate that
When the trainer would
Come out.

Get that little piece of wood
And twirl part of your uh . . .
Q-tip.

Yeah, and roll it back and
You feel like your eyeball's gonna
Drop out.

August 6, 1979
Baltimore at New York
Dennis Martinez pitching to Willie Randolph
Third inning, bases empty, one out
Orioles lead 1–0

Oklahoma

Boy I tell ya.
My geography for that part of the country
Is terrible.
Probably because there's a lot of snakes
Out there.
And I don't want to care to know too much
About that part of the country.
Two balls
One strike.
They got snakes in Oklahoma?
No?
No kiddin?
Great!

May 25, 1991 WPIX-TV
New York at Baltimore
Seventh inning, one out, bases empty
John Habyan pitching to Mike Devereaux
Score tied 3—3
Final: Yankees 5, Orioles 4

Phil Rizzuto

F.Y.I.

A little high.
Two balls
No strikes.

Riverview Medical Center
Is down the Jersey shore.

Three balls
No strikes.

> June 27, 1991 WPIX-TV
> New York at Boston
> Wade Taylor pitching to Tony Pena
> Seventh inning, no outs, bases empty
> Yankees lead 8–0
> Final: Yankees 8, Red Sox 0

Concord

Everything is named Walden up there.
Yeah.
Great poet.
Great great poet.
Another one . . .
Uh.
I gotta think of the other one up the—
It really is beautiful country.
I could very easily move up there.
I was thinking of Greenwich.
But I don't have enough money
To move up to Greenwich.
So I might move up to Concord.

September 20, 1991 WPIX-TV
New York at Boston
Scott Sanderson pitching to Scott Cooper
Seventh inning, two outs, bases empty
Red Sox lead 2–0
Final: Red Sox 2, Yankees 0

Phil Rizzuto

Paul Revere

I never knew that Paul Revere
Never made it to Concord.
He was ambushed right outside of Lexington.
And a fellow named Dawes picked up the—
It was almost like the Pony Express.
And he started out,
He didn't make it.
He got creamed
Somewhere between Lexington and Concord.
And then a fellow named Prescott
Finished it off.
And it's a strange thing.
But even in those days
You couldn't get a man to go nine.
Go the whole route.
You had to have a relief pitcher.
That is not a joke.
What was it?
It's not a good one.
Anyway . . .

> September 20, 1991 WPIX-TV
> New York at Boston
> Scott Sanderson pitching to Tom Brunansky
> Seventh inning, one out, bases empty
> Red Sox lead 2—0
> Final: Red Sox 2, Yankees 0

Bobby

I.

THE HAND FOR BOBBY MURCER!
WHO HAS FLIED TO CENTER AND WALKED.
BOBBY WILL BE
THE STARTING CENTER FIELDER
IN THE ALL-STAR GAME
TUESDAY NIGHT!

II.

YASTRZEMSKI STILL PLAYING
THAT VERY SHALLOW LEFT FIELD,
REGGIE SMITH WELL OVER IN RIGHT CENTER,
LAHOUD DEEP IN RIGHT!
KENNEY LEADS,
CULP'S PITCH!

Ground ball to second,
Could be two.
Kennedy goes to Aparicio.
Back to first.
Double play.

> July 11, 1971
> Boston at New York
> Ray Culp pitching to Bobby Murcer
> Fifth inning, one base runner, one out
> Red Sox lead 2–1

Mythkill

I'll say that a lot:
"Tonight,
We're going to Florida."
And they think
After the game
I fly to Florida.
And go down,
See the kids,
And come back the next day.

    May 30, 1992
    New York at Milwaukee
    Scott Sanderson pitching to Greg Vaughn
    Second inning, no outs, bases empty
    Yankees lead 3–0

Bubbles

I.
There's a restaurant up in Westchester
Called the Roman Gardens.
Joe DiMaggio loves that place.
Italian food.
Anyway,
Nat Racine,
One of the owners,
Had invited me up there for lunch.
Right?
What is that, Little Dave?
What are you pointing at?
I was trying to tell a story here
And you interrupted me.

II.
This is lunch don't forget.
All the sudden I sit down.
And Nat's . . .
I always start a story too late.
That's three out.
You want a game over that's quick?
Get the Scooter in here!
At the end of seven-and-a-half,
It's Toronto eleven and the Yankees one,
Now remember where I was, Seaver,
'Cause this is an unusual story.

Phil Rizzuto

III.

So . . .
Nat comes over and said,
Uhh.
And I didn't quite hear the whole sentence
That he said.
But he said,
He said,
Uhhhh.
All I heard was
"Don Perignon."
Right?

IV.

That's who I thought.
I had no idea.
And you know,
Lunch in the afternoon,
I figured . . .
So he poured me a glass.

And I'm not too much of a champagne drinker.
But I never did drink it.
Because every time I went to take a drink
The bubbles would hit me in the nose
And it felt so good
I just kept sitting there.
People must've thought I was nuts.

June 8, 1992
Toronto at New York
Lee Guetterman pitching to Jeff Kent
Top of the seventh, two outs, bases empty
Bob MacDonald pitching to Kevin Maas
Bottom of the seventh, no outs, bases empty
Blue Jays lead 11–1

Phil Rizzuto

California

It is weird out there.
California is kind of a weird state
Anyway . . .
I mean,
You go out there in the middle of the summer
And it's freezing.

> June 9, 1992
> Toronto at New York
> Juan Guzman pitching to Charlie Hayes
> Fifth inning, no outs, bases empty
> Score tied 1–1

Greenwich Time

I.

Had a great time up in Greenwich.
It's a nice little town.
And you know,
You know what I like, Seaver,
About that town?
You can get two hours
On those meters in town.

II.

I got a ticket up in Windsor.
I parked for an hour and a half
And I had put money in it,
But they mark your tire
With the chalk mark.
I didn't know that.

III.

You're only allowed to stay an hour.
And I find I had to go to a county clerk
In a little wooden shack.
Pay 'em five dollars.

IV.

That's the only bad thing about Greenwich.
They don't have any parking areas.

Phil Rizzuto

You gotta wait for somebody
To pull out of a parking spot.

> June 20, 1992
> New York at Baltimore
> Jeff Johnson pitching to Leo Gomez
> Third inning, one out, bases empty
> Yankees lead 6–4

Lake Effect

They had a warning out.
I was watching the television.
And they had that crawl underneath.
There was a—
No.
Not frostbite.
But they had water spouts
Coming up in Lake . . .
Uh—
Lake Michigan.
What is it?
Lake Michigan?
It's not Lake Michigan.
Is it?

      August 14, 1992
      New York at Chicago
      Scott Kamieniecki pitching to George Bell
      Second inning, no outs, bases empty
      No score

Colorado

They're having more snow
Out in Colorado.
Which is not in Montana.
But it is not far from Montana.

August 26, 1992
Milwaukee at New York
Sam Militello pitching to Darryl Hamilton
Third inning, one out, bases empty
Brewers lead 1–0

Beaches

We don't have them here.
It's out in California.

Oklahoma doesn't have them.
You got any beaches in Oklahoma?

> August 9, 1992
> Boston at New York
> Sam Militello pitching to Jack Clark
> Second inning, no outs, bases empty
> Yankees lead 3—0

Phil Rizzuto

Zamboanga

When I was in the service
In the Philippines
I was in Zamboanga for a few days.
Fortunately,
I got out of there.
At the time
There was nothing there
But coconut trees.

> August 28, 1992
> New York at Minnesota
> Scott Erickson pitching to Randy Velarde
> Fourth inning, no outs, bases empty
> Twins lead 1—0

This Planet Warm and Human

Mia.
Now Mia's been a very popular
Name in the newspapers lately,
Murcer.
I mean.

That took the headline.
Unbelievable!
Only in New York
Would it take the headlines away.
Yeah.

Unbelievable.
Terrible.
Terrible what's happening in that situation
And with all that going on down in Florida.
Boy.

They're still showing those pictures on TV
Of the damage down in Florida
By the way,
Are we going to Florida today,
Moore?
O that's in for a base hit!
Two runs will score!
No they won't.

Phil Rizzuto

August 30, 1992
New York at Minnesota
Sam Militello pitching to Brian Harper
Fourth inning, one out, two base runners
(Single scores one run)
Twins lead 1–0

Luck of the Irish

I can get this story in.
'Cause I just came back from Rochester.
I just started to talk about Joe Altobelli up in Rochester.
And Johnny Antonelli who lives in Rochester.
They have an Italian Open up there
For the benefit of the Boys and Girls Town of Italy.
And I mean,
The town is loaded with Italians.
Those beautiful names,
All ending in vowels that slip on . . .
O wonderful people!
Very . . .
Every once in a while,
An Irish,
Ryan or something
Would get in there.
Would just kind of break the melody
Of the Italian names.
And who do you think won the tournament?
There was like 200 Italians and about six Irishmen.
The Irishmen won.
LINED TO RIGHT,
AND DIVING . . .
IT'S BY HIM!
GROUND RULE DOUBLE!

Phil Rizzuto

September 15, 1992
Chicago at New York
Rich Monteleone pitching to Steve Sax
Eighth inning, one out, one base runner
Yankees lead 2–1

These Heaters

They're no good.
Because at my height
It goes over my head
And hits the guys in back of me.

I mean . . .

They were not built,
These heaters were not built
For normal human beings.
They were built for people like Seaver.

> April 27, 1992
> Texas at New York
> Scott Sanderson pitching to Geno Petralli
> Fourth inning, one out, one base runner
> Yankees lead 3–1

Phil Rizzuto

Buccinator Novi Temporis

I tell ya . . .
The last two days
The weather has been
Absolutely beautiful.
Right now,
There's something wrong.
My nose is getting stuffed up.
It almost feels like rain.
Doesn't it?

> August 22, 1992
> California at New York
> Chuck Finley pitching to Roberto Kelly
> Third inning, no outs, one base runner
> No score

Glasses

It seems like when we were playing, Jerry,
Only the outfielders wore them
And seldom maybe rarely the infielders wore them.
There's a strike to Howser.
And I think that it takes a lot of getting used to.
If you flip them down too quick, you're in trouble.
And if you flip them down too late, you're in trouble.
It's quite an art of flipping down those glasses.
The runners lead off first and second.
The pitch to Howser,
Swing and a foul tip, strike two.
Actually if the glasses are oiled up properly,
You just flip the tip of your cap.
You don't even have to touch the glasses and they'll fall
    down.
But if you have to flip two or three times,
And you're not following that ball,
When you flip them down,
As Jerry says, suddenly everything gets dark.

> May 21, 1967
> New York at Detroit
> Earl Wilson pitching to Dick Howser
> Sixth inning, two base runners, two out
> Tigers lead 7—0

Phil Rizzuto

My Nose

Now,
You wouldn't believe this!
When you were a kid,
Did you ever have those fights,
You would get on
On your buddy's back . . .
We called them elephant fights.
I don't know why.
We'd be elephant.
It'd be like Johnny on a Pony.
You get on
And you try to pull the other guy off
The other guy's back.
This was a game we played in Brooklyn.
And this kid swang around to get me,
Hit me with his elbow in the nose,
And I went to the teach,
And said,
"I think my nose is broken."
She said,
"No, it's not."
And she wouldn't let me go home.
No.
No, it is NOT!
Not snot.
And she wouldn't let me go home.

And then it was too late to set the nose.
GOOD PLAY BY MAAS!

> August 19, 1991 WPIX-TV
> Kansas City at New York
> Mike Boddicker pitching to Randy Velarde
> Eighth inning, two outs, two base runners
> Score tied 2–2
> Final: Yankees 6, Royals 2

Phil Rizzuto

Dream Day

It turned out to be
One of the most beautiful days.
I had no idea
I was going to play golf today.
I didn't bring any shoes.
Or balls.
Or glove.
Or clothes.
But they . . .
They gave me a full complement.
And I was very embarrassed to take it.

> May 26, 1992
> New York at Minnesota
> Pat Mahomes pitching to Mel Hall
> First inning, one out, one base runner
> Yankees lead 1—0

Symmetry

I wanna tell ya.
They replayed that game.
I got a chance to see it.
On MSG last night.
Man.
I mean,
Every game,
As you mentioned,
In Milwaukee
Was an exciting ball game.
They won two ball games
We should've won.
And we won two ball games
They should've won.
UNBELIEVABLE!

> May 26, 1992
> New York at Minnesota
> Pat Mahomes pitching to Mike Gallego
> First inning, no outs, bases empty
> No score

Phil Rizzuto

Wait a Minute

Wait a minute.
Wait a—
You can't call him "Scooter"
With me in the booth,
Seaver.
That name is . . .
That name is patented.

> May 30, 1992
> New York at Chicago
> Scott Sanderson pitching to Jim Gantner
> Third inning, one out, one base runner
> Yankees lead 3–0

Ticktock, the Clock

Whatever happened
To the days
When the catchers
Throw the ball
To the pitcher?
Get the sign,
Wind up,
And throw.
I can't believe
How much time
They take.

> June 5, 1992
> Detroit at New York
> Scott Sanderson pitching to Tony Phillips
> Eighth inning, one out, one base runner
> Tigers lead 4–2

Phil Rizzuto

Mattingly's Surprise

That's deep!
Down the left field line!
And gonna currrrrrve.
HOLY COW!
A HOME RUN!
Ho ho ho.
RIGHT DOWN THE LINE!
LOOK:
Even Mattingly is surprised.

> May 30, 1992
> New York at Milwaukee
> Chris Bosio pitching to Don Mattingly
> Fourth inning, one out, two men on
> Double
> Yankees lead 8—0

Unwashed

I wouldn't eat anything now
After watching that bug walk on his hand.
I wouldn't shake hands with him either.

> July 9, 1992
> Seattle at New York
> Greg Cadaret pitching to Tino Martinez
> Eighth inning, no outs, one base runner
> Yankees lead 7–5

Phil Rizzuto

Go Ahead, Seaver

You know,
Some kid wrote me a letter.
You and Murcer,
I know,
Every time Murcer says
I make oh for four and two errors.
Some guy wrote,
Which I haven't gotten yet,
He wrote it to Yankee Stadium,
But by the way,
You're doing the play-by-play, Seaver.
So go ahead.
I was gonna tell you something,
But I forgot what it was.
Go ahead.

> July 1, 1991 WPIX-TV
> Cleveland at New York
> Lee Guetterman pitching to Chris James
> Seventh inning, no outs, bases empty
> Yankees lead 6–2

Thought for Seaver

It's funny
How certain words
In the English language
Could be very confusing.
You just said,
"They're idle this week."
Now you were an idol
Of all the kids at USC.
And it's spelled differently.
Idle and idol.
I just thought of that.

> Sept. 7, 1991
> New York at Minnesota
> Pascual Perez pitching to Greg Gagne
> Fifth inning, two outs, bases empty
> Yankees lead 1–0

Phil Rizzuto

Instructions for the World

Watch this.
Forget about the script.
Don't read.
Don't read.
Ad-lib it.
And I had it upside down.

> May 30, 1992
> New York at Milwaukee
> Scott Sanderson pitching to Scott Fletcher
> Third inning, one out, bases empty
> Showing Bob Uecker in another booth
> Yankees lead 3–0

Reversal of Opinion

And he hits one in the hole
They're gonna have to hurry.
THEY'LL NEVER GET HIM!
They got him.
How do you like that.
Holy cow.
I changed my mind before he got there.
So that doesn't count as an error.

> July 10, 1992
> Seattle at New York
> Dave Fleming pitching to Andy Stankiewicz
> First inning, no outs, bases empty
> Mariners lead 1–0

Phil Rizzuto

Observation

You know,
I was just thinking.
It's tough
To evaluate players
When you're out
On the golf course.

August 14, 1992
New York at Chicago
Alex Fernandez pitching to Matt Nokes
Seventh inning, two outs, bases empty
White Sox lead 2—0

To Blow a Story

I was talking with Sam McDowell.
You know Sam.
Great left-handed pitcher.
Very wild on and off the field.
Now he has settled down.
Does a great job.
Oh,
He's got his own clinic.
Anyway,
He told me that Bob Feller was popping off.
About how many pitches
He threw in one game.
Two hundred and sixty pitches.
McDowell said,
"Forget it!"
He threw two hundred NINETY pitches
In one inning.
Oh no . . .
Oh see . . .
I blew the . . .
I messed the . . .
Two hundred ninety pitches . . .
Not an inning.
I made a mistake.
I did.
I blew the story.
And it was a good story.

August 31, 1991, WPIX-TV
Toronto at New York
Greg Cadaret pitching to Roberto Alomar
Seventh inning, bases empty, no outs
Blue Jays lead 1–0
Final: Blue Jays 5, Yankees 0

To Finish a Story

One of the most embarrassing moments
In Mel Allen's life,
Not mine,
Was the day Mel and I
Were doing the game
At Cleveland's Municipal Stadium.
And the television booth
Was way on the third base side.
You talk about the game
While I finish this story.
And the radio was on the first base side,
And at the end of four and a half innings
We'd have to change positions.
The game started.
And McDowell was supposed to pitch.
And we said,
"McDowell's pitching!"
For seven innings
We had McDowell pitching.
Don't you go in on me,
Seaver.
This story's gonna be good by the end.
They got him!
Two outs.
I'm gonna finish this story.
Let me just finish this story.
In the seventh inning
Somebody calls from New York

Phil Rizzuto

Watching the game on PIX.
They said,
"That's not McDowell pitching.
"That's Kralick."
I laughed.
But Mel Allen wanted to throw
Our statistician out of the booth.
Poor Bill Kane.
He threw pencils at him.
Books at him.
Holy cow.

August 31, 1991 WPIX-TV
Toronto at New York
Greg Cadaret pitching to Joe Carter
Seventh inning, bases empty, two outs
(Carter grounds out to Espinoza)
Blue Jays 1, Yankees 0
Final: Blue Jays 5, Yankees 0

Doom Balloon

Another balloon coming our way,
Seaver.
Must be a down-draft
Right here.
Pink balloon.
THAT SON OF A GUN'S COMING RIGHT—

> August 14, 1992
> New York at Chicago
> Alex Fernandez pitching to Charlie Hayes
> Third inning, two outs, bases empty
> White Sox lead 1–0

Phil Rizzuto

Brew

Anyway . . .
Brew and I,
As I said,
We played 36
Holes of golf.
And if you ever
Saw Brew eat,
I mean,
He can eat.

August 7, 1992 WPIX–TV
Boston at New York
Scott Sanderson pitching to Scott Cooper
Seventh inning, two outs, bases empty
Yankees lead 4–0

Very Frustrated

I tell ya,
I tried that new McLean burger.
Very good.

Of course,
My cholesterol is very high.
Very high.

> August 5, 1991
> New York at Detroit
> Jerry Don Gleaton pitching to Pat Kelly
> Ninth inning, no outs, bases empty
> Yankees lead 7—5

Phil Rizzuto

I, Witness

You wanna see
Somebody butcher
A cheesecake?

You should see
Seaver and Brewer up here.
Holy cow!

> June 5, 1992
> Detroit at New York
> Sixth inning, two outs, one base runner
> Tigers lead 4–2

The Indelible Smell

What kind is it?
Ohhhhh!
Pepperoni!
Holy cow!
What happened?
Base hit!
A little disconcerting,
Smelling that pizza,
And trying
To do a ball game.

> August 19, 1992
> Oakland at New York
> Mike Moore pitching to Charlie Hayes
> Sixth inning, one out, bases empty
> Yankees lead 4–1

Phil Rizzuto

Asylum

Got some chocolate chip cookies here,
Murcer.
So don't ask me any questions
For a batter or so.
All right?

> June 17, 1992
> New York at Boston
> Roger Clemens pitching to Mel Hall
> Sixth inning, two outs, bases empty
> Red Sox lead 2—1

To the Rescue

And here comes John Amarante,
Who sang the national anthem,
With cannolis!

Put 'em there.
O, thank you, John.
We will enjoy it.

> July 24, 1983 (The Pine Tar Game)
> Kansas City at New York
> Bud Black pitching to Bert Campaneris
> First inning, bases empty, no outs.
> No score.

Phil Rizzuto

Bearing Down

One strike on him.
Gotta bear down here.

Gotta get this kid
Out of the jam.

Wanna see him pitch
A shutout today.

      August 9, 1992
      Boston at New York
      Sam Militello pitching to Herm Winningham
      Second inning, no outs, one base runner
      Yankees lead 3–0

If

It's deep to right.
But not far enough.
Tartabull is back.
Makes the catch.

O, I'm tellin' ya,
That would have been
Some long home run
If he'd just hit it square.

> April 13, 1991
> New York at Kansas City
> Bret Saberhagen pitching to Torey Lovullo
> Third inning, no outs, bases empty
> Royals lead 2–0

Phil Rizzuto

Possessions

Sanderson practicing the forkball.
Is that the new kid with him?
The new kid on the block?
Bob Wickman?
Yeah.
He wants the ball.
Sanderson won't give him the ball!
GIVE HIM THE BALL!
Foul back and out of play.

> August 26, 1992
> Milwaukee at New York
> Bill Wegman pitching to Randy Velarde
> Second inning, one out, bases empty
> Brewers lead 1—0
> Final: Yankees 4, Brewers 3

Surprise Attack

OH NOW!
SEAVER!
WITH THOSE STRONG FINGERS!
HE—
GAHHH!
HE JUST TAPS YOU ON THE BACK.
AND YOU'RE BLACK AND BLUE.
GAHHH!
COME ON!

September 4, 1992
Texas at New York
Matt Whiteside pitching to Mel Hall
Sixth inning, one out, one base runner
Yankees lead 6—3

Phil Rizzuto

Chess

I.

A lot of money in that chess.
I'll tell you that.
It's gotta be . . .
Can't be . . .
Not a good game for television.

II.

I'm not knocking it.
But it's not a spectator sport.

> September 4, 1992
> Texas at New York
> Rich Monteleone pitching to Rafael Palmeiro
> Seventh inning, no outs, bases empty
> Yankees lead 6–3

Hall and Nokes

So second time around
Mel Hall and Matt Nokes
Solve Tapani's pitch.
Heh heh.
That's right.
John Moore's on the ball.
It does sound like a good rock group.
Hall and Nokes.
Oh?
Hall and Oates?
Oh yeah?
That's one I missed.
I'll have to go out
And buy some of their records tonight.

> June 11, 1991
> New York at Minnesota
> Kevin Tapani pitching to Alvaro Espinoza
> Fifth inning, two outs, two base runners
> Twins lead 1—0

Phil Rizzuto

The Prince

I.
Last night I was watching TV.
I was watching Arsenio Hall.
And he had Prince on.
I wanna—
What a character he is!
Holy cow!

II.
Entertainer.
Singer.
And he can dance.
He's a little bitty guy.
He had a weird beard.
I tell ya it was—
I couldn't explain it.

III.
It was a real beard.
I mean,
You know how they do it now.
Some of them.
It doesn't come all the way
Up to the sideburns.
It starts,

Then it goes.
You gotta see it to believe it.

> Sept. 10, 1991
> New York at Baltimore
> Eric Plunk pitching to Bill Ripken
> Second inning, one out, one base runner
> Yankees lead 2–1
> Final: Orioles 6, Yankees 3

Polonia's Hair

I.
Look it.
I gotta tell my barber on Monday,
"Don't gimme a Polonia haircut."
Holy Cow!

II.
That's the latest style.
It's just like
When new styles come out for women.
They wear it no matter how weird it looks.
They'll wear it 'cause it's a new style.

III.
Gonna get the women mad at me.
I'll think of something.
What?
I got another half minute
To think of something
To get out of this.

August 22, 1992
California at New York
Melido Perez pitching to Luis Sojo
Sixth inning, two outs, one base runner
Yankees lead 2—0
Final: Yankees 3, Angels 0

Mere Anarchy Is Loosed Upon the World

I tell ya.
Before long,
Football starts.
This weekend
In seriousness.
And pretty soon
It'll be hockey
And then basketball.
And then baseball
Will still
Be going on.
And it'll be
Very confusing.
Very confusing.

> August 31, 1991 WPIX-TV
> Toronto at New York
> Mike Timlin pitching to Pat Sheridan
> Eighth inning, bases empty, one out
> Blue Jays lead 2—0
> Final: Blue Jays 5, Yankees 0

Phil Rizzuto

I Stuck My Hand In

Everything I tried to do turned out bad.
I tried to run a snowblower.
I stuck my hand in
And cut some of my fingers off.

I mean, I'm lucky I can turn on the car
And know how it runs.

If I open the refrigerator,
And it's not right in front of me,
I don't know what I'm looking for.
I mean, it's terrible.

> July 31, 1994
> Cooperstown, New York
> Major League Baseball Hall of Fame Induction

Apodosis

Fly ball right field
It's gonna drop in.
No it's not gonna drop in.
Happy 46th wedding anniversary
Thomas and Mary Anne Clearwater.
That's it.
The last three, six, nine, twelve Yankees
Went down in order.
So that's it.
The game is over.

> June 4, 1991
> Toronto at New York
> Tom Henke pitching to Pat Kelly
> Ninth inning, two outs, bases empty
> Toronto wins 5—3

Phil Rizzuto

Scooter at the Bat

BY FRANK CAMMUSO AND HART SEELY

This piece appeared in the New York Times *on October 16, 1993, as the mighty Philadelphia Phillies and Toronto Blue Jays prepared to square off in the World Series. Next day, Phil called to thank us. He said he'd been ill, and it raised his spirits.*

The outlook wasn't brilliant for the Mudville nine that day;
The score stood four to two, with but one inning more to play;
Hey Murcer! Who's got play-by-play? You? No? *I do*?
Those last two outs I been sitting here, thinking it was you.

A straggling few got up to go in deep despair. The rest
Clung to the hope which springs eternal in the human breast.
Time out. A fan running out on the field. You hate to see that.
They'd put up even money now, with Casey at the bat.

But Flynn preceded Casey, as did also Jimmy Blake.
Seeing that fan just reminded me of something, Seaver.
I think I got time to get this story in.
Joe Altobelli and Johnny Antonelli, who live in Rochester,
They got an Italian Open up there every year.
Hey look, TELLY SAVALAS! Almost missed him in that hat.
For there seemed but little chance of Casey's getting to
the bat.

But Flynn let drive a single, to the wonderment of all.
It's a tournament to benefit the Boys and Girls Towns of Italy.

O Holy Cow! 169

And I mean, that whole town is loaded with Italians.

So I—lined to left, I THINK THAT'S GONNA FALL.

And Blake, the much despised, tore the cover off the ball;

Down the line. ATTA-BOY, JIMMY. Up against the wall!

You know, Seaver. I saw Ted Williams the other day,

He made this remark, and I'm not saying it

Because I agree with him wholeheartedly.

But he said, "Pitchers are the dumbest ballplayers.

'Cause all they know how to do is pitch."

So I'm asking you, what did you think of that statement?

I'm asking you a simple question, Seaver.

Tom Seaver here is not answering me. Not a word.

There was Jimmy safe on second, and Flynn a-hugging third.

Then from the gladdened multitude went up a joyous yell

Anyway, what was I saying when we got those hits?

Rochester! Gotta keep talking about Rochester.

Gotta keep this rally going, Seaver.

So, you know, one thing about Rochester . . .

They'll ticket your car if you're gone for a minute.

I tell ya. They got the highway patrols out.

And look who's up. Holy cow. How do you like that!

For Casey, mighty Casey, was advancing to the bat.

There was ease in Casey's manner as he stepped into his place.

Hey, Murcer, know what's on tonight after the game?

Pro wrestling! I mean, it's a great sport.

I used to know all the old-time wrestlers.

A lot of people, you know, they think it's all fixed.

I just don't know about that.

No stranger in the crowd could doubt 'twas Casey at the bat.

Phil Rizzuto

Ten thousand eyes were on him as he rubbed his hands
    with dirt.
Small crowd tonight, Seaver, considering it's a pennant race.
I tell ya. Anyway, back in Rochester.
All those Italian names in that golf tournament,
Every once in a while, an Irish, a Ryan or something
Would get in there, just kind of break up the melody.
There was like 200 Italians and about six Irishmen.
And who do you think won? The Irishmen won.
Unbelievable.

And now the leather-covered sphere came hurtling
    through the air.
Hey, you wanna see somebody butcher a cheesecake!
You should see Murcer and Seaver up here.
That's a ball, outside. You'd think they're never fed.
"That ain't my style," said Casey. "Strike one," the umpire said.
STRIKE? I don't believe it. I'm gonna have to take my pill.
Crowd really getting on home plate umpire Derwood Merrill.
Let's see that on replay. Look at that! I just don't
    understand . . .
And it's likely they'd have killed him had not Casey raised
    his hand.
With a smile of Christian charity great Casey's visage
    shone;
Hey Murcer, you ever play chess?
A lot of money in that chess, you know. I tell ya.
A lot of money. But it's not a good game for television.
I'm not knocking it, but it's not a spectator sport.
Breaking ball. High and inside. Oooooh.
But Casey still ignored it, and the umpire said, "Strike two."

"Fraud!" cried the maddened thousands, and the echo
   answered "Fraud!"
Hey, Murcer! Look! BEA ARTHUR! Didn't she play Maude?
Anyway. Back to Rochester. Gotta get these two runs in.
And they knew that Casey wouldn't let that ball go by again.

The sneer is gone from Casey's lips, his teeth are clenched
   in hate.
You know, Murcer, I had in Rochester the best meal I ever ate.
And now the pitcher holds the ball, and now he lets it go.
OH! THAT'S GONE! HOLY COW! OHHH . . . no . . .

Oh! Somewhere in this favored land, the sun is shining bright
Wait a minute. What happened? I lost it in the light.
Happy Birthday, Gene Paluzzi, who I hear has got the gout . . .
But there is no joy in Mudville—mighty Casey has struck out.

Afterword

BY HART SEELY AND TOM PEYER

During the late 1980s, baseball fans called the New York Yan-kees "the worst team money could buy"—an affront to the team's proud heritage, if not to all of humanity. For about ten years, rooting for the Bombers was like watching a great man-sion fall apart due to neglect.

But Yankee fans enjoyed one secret pleasure. For three innings each night, we could hear Phil Rizzuto expound on the vagaries of everyday life. Each game might bring an update on a certain cannoli that crossed his path, a town he played golf in, or a postcard from a friend. Of course, any Riz-zutonian story might go unfinished, sudden victim to the inning-ending double play. But wasn't that life?

Next day, you'd see a fellow Yankee diehard and recite not how the team lost, but what Scooter said. We came to know Phil as an old friend—not a retired jock or a professional talk-ing head. He was a real person, just talking about his life.

This is not to put down the announcers of today. They hone their craft, develop their styles, and can report each batter's slugging percentage against left-handed pitchers with runners on base in the month of July. They tell the score, stick to the program, and shout out with heartfelt emotion when it's their job to do so.

The Scooter, though, would tell of his trip to Rochester.

His world consisted of good people. Even Red Sox fans celebrated birthdays. He called coworkers by last names—"Hey, Seaver! Hey, Murcer! Hey, White!"—a manner that today would sound gruff yet, with Phil, only imparted boundless friendship. He celebrated every Yankee accomplishment not with a stock phrase but by joyously appreciating its place in the universe. And when bad things occurred in this world, Phil did not hide his remorse. The night after Thurman Munson died, he prayed on the air. Could any other play-by-play announcer have done that?

In 1991 our weekly "Poetry of P. F. Rizzuto" began appearing in the *Village Voice*. They were edgy pieces, the kind of humor that a less-secure public figure might denounce. At first, Phil wasn't sure what to make of it. Later, he told the publisher he'd given it a litmus test: He asked Yogi, and Yogi laughed. And so a book came into being.

Two years later, with *O Holy Cow!* in the stores and yet-another lost Yankee season concluding, we finally got a chance to meet Phil. We were to appear with him for a half-inning on a WPIX-TV Yankee broadcast. We arrived an hour early. Phil shook our hands and thanked us for the book, though he noted that the best poetry always rhymes.

We found our seats, then watched the heavens open. Our epitaphs shall read: YANKEE TV APPEARANCE RAINED OUT.

Of course, we already knew that even a great story can get cut by the inning-ending double play.

The morning of August 14, 2007, e-mails began to arrive, offering condolences. The Scooter had passed away. We phoned each other, trying to decide what to say. Soon, reporters were calling, asking for insights into Phil Rizzuto, the poet. We didn't really have any. Upon reflection, we offer this:

Phil Rizzuto's greatest poetry is not this book. It is the fundamental goodness of a man who lived a long, fruitful life and never lost his innocence.

These days, the Yanks always make the playoffs, teams wish fans happy birthdays on giant scoreboards, and we always know the slugging percentages against left-handed pitchers during the month of July. Maybe that's progress. But it's not the same. We'll miss those trips to Rochester.

In that regard, we hope these verses bear testimony to an old friend who just happened to be a Yankee great and Hall of Fame shortstop, a fellow named Phil, who loved to tell about his life and times.

And that, of course, is the greatest poetry of all.

Publisher's Note

The Phil Rizzuto Estate has donated all royalties from *O Holy Cow! The Selected Verse of Phil Rizzuto* to a variety of children's charities, including Saint Joseph's School for the Blind in Jersey City, New Jersey, the Hale House Center in New York City, and the Children's Specialized Hospital in Mountainside, New Jersey.